Ellen Catala

Contents

Rigby®

A Harcourt Achieve Imprint

www.Rigby.com

1-800-531-5015

Charles and Amelia

Charles Lindbergh and Amelia Earhart
had the same dream.
They wanted to fly airplanes
to places far away.

In 1927 Charles decided to fly his small plane across the Atlantic Ocean. He began his long flight in New York. He flew all the way to Paris, France! It took him almost 34 hours.

Charles's Flight

New York

34 hour flight

Paris

Atlantic Ocean

N
W E
S

In 1932 Amelia decided to fly her small plane across the Atlantic Ocean. She began her flight in Newfoundland. She landed in Ireland after flying through strong winds and rain.

It took her almost 15 hours!

Amelia's Flight

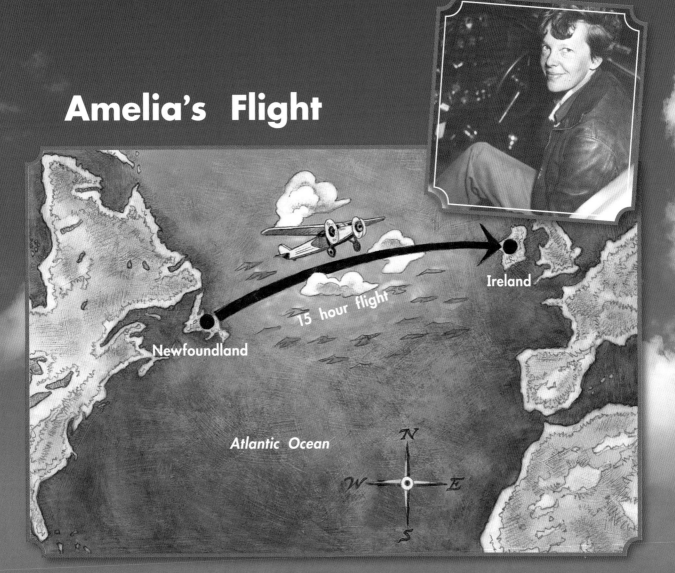

Newfoundland

15 hour flight

Ireland

Atlantic Ocean

N
W · E
S

Honors

People called Charles "Lucky Lindy"
because he won a lot of prizes.
Charles won prizes because
he was so brave.
He even won a special prize
called the "Medal of Valor."

People thought Amelia was very brave, too.

Parades were held to honor her.

More than 3,400 people showed up

at a parade in Kansas to honor her.

They all wanted to see their hero, Amelia!

Our Heroes

Charles became the first man to fly by himself across the Atlantic Ocean.

Amelia became the first woman who did the same thing.

They both proved that anything was possible.

Charles and Amelia were very brave and didn't let anything stop them. They made many people everywhere very happy.

That is why we call them our heroes in the sky!